Engineering Design Notebook

elevate science

Pearson Education, Inc. 330 Hudson Street, New York, NY 10013

© Pearson Education, Inc., or its affiliates. All Rights Reserved. Printed in the United States of America.

This publication is protected by copyright, and permission should be obtained from the publisher prior to any prohibited reproduction, storage in a retrieval system, or transmission in any form or by any means, electronic, mechanical, photocopying, recording, or otherwise. For information regarding permissions, request forms, and the appropriate contacts within the Pearson Education Global Rights & Permissions Department, please visit www.pearsoned.com/permissions/.

PEARSON and ALWAYS LEARNING are exclusive trademarks owned by Pearson Education, Inc. or its affiliates in the United States and/or other countries.

Unless otherwise indicated herein, any third-party trademarks that may appear in this work are the property of their respective owners and any references to third-party trademarks, logos, or other trade dress are for demonstrative or descriptive purposes only. Such references are not intended to imply any sponsorship, endorsement, authorization, or promotion of Pearson's products by the owners of such marks, or any relationship between the owner and Pearson Education, Inc. or its affiliates, authors, licensees, or its affiliates, authors, licensees or distributors.

ISBN-13:   978-0-32-895387-5
ISBN-10:   0-32-895387-3

1 18

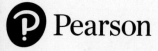 Pearson

Boston, Massachusetts   Chandler, Arizona
Glenview, Illinois   New York, New York

TABLE OF CONTENTS

The Engineering Design Process iv

Topic 1 Living Things in the Biosphere
Attack of the Viruses! viii

Topic 2 The Cell System
A Tree With Superpowers 4

Topic 3 Human Body Systems
Engineering an Organ 8

Topic 4 Reproduction and Growth
Build a Plant Growth Chamber 12

Topic 5 Ecosystems
Put Decomposers to Work at Home 16

Topic 6 Populations, Communities, and Ecosystems
Building a Dome 20

Topic 7 Genes and Heredity
Develop a Secret Code 24

Topic 8 Natural Selection and Change Over Time
Way to Dig! 28

The Engineering and Design Process

An engineer is a person who designs, builds, and/or maintains machines, structures, or systems. Typically, an engineer is sought when a problem has to be solved or a new structure needs to be built to certain specifications. Engineers can specialize in many different disciplines, and include civil engineers, electrical engineers, chemical engineers, and environmental engineers.

Engineers follow a process to develop a new product or system that meets a human need or want. This process is called the engineering design process. Within this process, they use scientific and technological knowledge to meet the requirements of whatever project they are working on.

Just as in the process of completing a scientific experiment, the steps in the engineering and design process do not have to follow a certain order. At any stage of the process a new problem may be discovered and new solutions can be generated, tested, and evaluated for success. This causes the steps of the process to overlap and feedback into other steps. Throughout the design process, engineers should use scientific reasoning, document procedures and results, and communicate with those people who will evaluate and rely on the designed solution.

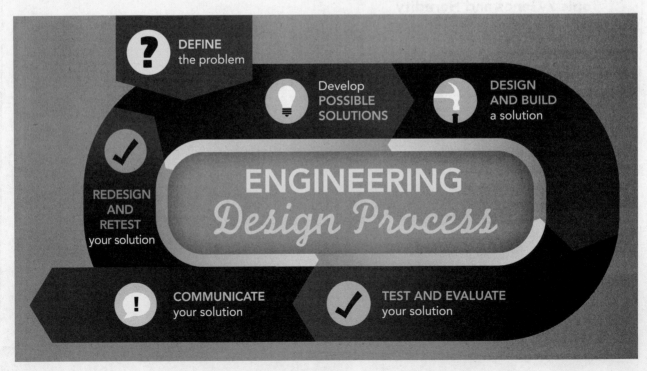

Define the Problem

Identifying the problem that can be solved through engineering involves more than simply stating the function of the device or system that is being designed. Identifying the problem includes identifying the basic need that the solution needs to address and how to determine if the solution is successful or not. Engineers must also account for unintended impacts on society or the environment when defining the problem.

One way to detail a problem is to list criteria and constraints for a project. Criteria and constraints are similar but distinct terms. A criteria is an attribute that the design must have in order to be successful. A constraint is a limitation that the solution must accommodate. Look at the examples in the table of possible criteria and constraints for an egg drop activity to see the difference between criteria and constraints.

Sample Criteria and Constraints Table	
Criteria	**Constraints**
• The design solution must allow an uncooked egg to remain intact when the device impacts the ground. • The solution must protect the egg on all drops from a height of 3 meters or less. • The egg must be able to be inserted and removed from the device without breaking or taking apart the device. • The device itself should be able to handle repeated drops without needing repairs.	• The design solution must only make use of materials provided by the teacher. • The solution must be built within 45 minutes. • The solution may not make use of a parachute. • Member of the group may not consult people in other groups or people outside of the classroom. • The solution must fit inside a regular-sized shoebox without being taken apart.

Develop Possible Solutions

Engineers often collaborate with other engineers to brainstorm possible solutions and research various types of materials. Gathering and researching information help engineers compare possible and existing solutions. As the design team works, the members record and document the information they gather and the ideas they generate.

Because this stage of the process is brainstorming, any and all ideas should be encouraged and pursued. The people collaborating on the process should be allowed to let creativity spark as many different solutions as possible. Having a larger variety of solutions to choose from and compare with each other will make it more likely that the most ideal solution is found during the evaluation process.

Design a Solution

Engineers use the information from their research and brainstorming ideas to choose possible solutions to develop further. Materials are selected to build their design solutions. Plans are checked against criteria and constraints to ensure their suitability.

Designed solutions can take many different forms. They can include zprototypes (physical or working models), drawings (conceptual models or blueprints), computer models, and mathematical models.

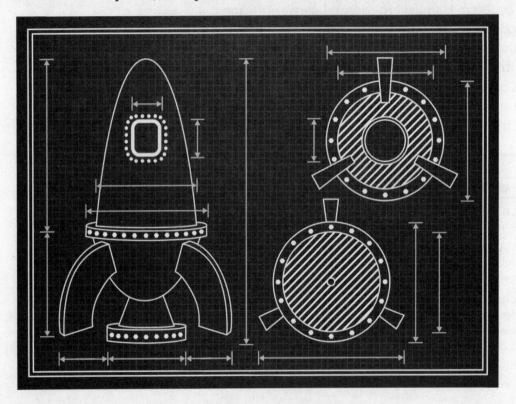

Test and Evaluate a Solution

Engineers plan and carry out investigations to build and test prototypes and design solutions. The prototype or new design solution is evaluated against criteria and constraints. Engineers use systematic methods to compare different solutions to see which best meet criteria and constraints, and compare measurable data.

One method of evaluation is to compare a solution to the criteria to see how well the criteria are met, and the constraints to make sure the solution stayed within the limits defined by the constraints. Numerical criteria can be evaluated by running repeated trials and collecting data to get as much precision and accuracy in the test results as possible.

Solutions may also be tested by building models. For example, placing a newly formed design for a vehicle in a wind tunnel will allow you to collect data about properties such as speed, drag, and efficiency.

Communicate the Solution

The design team needs to communicate the final design to the people who will use and manufacture the new product. Engineers critically read and evaluate scientific and technical texts to support and communicate their design solutions.

This communication often leads to feedback that will result in a redesign or request for modifications to the solution. This can cause the engineering team to solve a new problem with a different set of criteria and constraints, or it may simply result in modifications to the design and more testing.

Redesign and Retest the Solution

Engineers test and revise solutions a number of times in order to arrive at an optimal design while considering the limits of the prototype or new design solution. They also combine parts of different solutions to create new solutions.

In order to perform this step successfully, engineers must develop rigorous methods to compare different solutions and integrate their testing data into the prototypes or models that they have designed.

Attack of the Viruses!

Viruses cannot survive by themselves. Unlike bacterial or human cells, viruses lack the ability to multiply and create new viruses. So, they have to use a host—bacteria, human, or animal—to use as a temporary home in which to grow and multiply.

Viruses multiply by attaching themselves to a host cell and injecting their DNA or RNA into it. The virus uses the cell to create copies of itself. The copies then move on to new cells to invade and infect.

A bacteriophage is a type of virus that attacks bacteria. The virus uses its tail fibers almost like legs to land on a bacterial cell. Then it lowers the end of its tail onto the outer surface of the cell. Finally, it injects its DNA from its head through its tail into the cell.

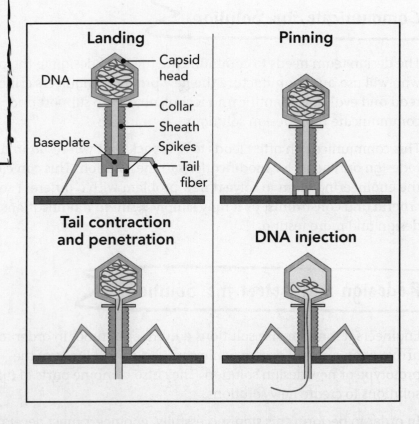

DESIGN CHALLENGE

The World Health Organization (WHO) has approached your class to help raise global awareness about infectious agents such as viruses. As part of the project, the WHO is hoping that you can construct a working model of a virus to teach children and adults around the world about the dangers of these microscopic invaders.

How can you use everyday objects to construct your model? How will your model function to mimic the action of a virus as it infects a cell?

Define Your Problem

1. To come up with an effective design for your virus model, you need to consider the problem you are trying to solve. How does the structure of the virus allow it to successfully multiply? Define your problem and identify a possible design solution for your virus model.

....

....

....

Identify Design Criteria/Constraints

Criteria

☐ Your model must accurately represent the different parts of a virus.

☐ The model must show how a virus attacks and infects a cell.

Constraints

☐ The model must be made from readily available materials in your classroom.

☐ You have 30 minutes to plan and construct your model.

Consider art supplies such as clay, construction paper, craft sticks, pipe cleaners, plastic piping, cardboard tubes, wire, rubber balls, or balloons.

2. Given these constraints and criteria, how must your design work to effectively demonstrate how a virus attacks a host cell and multiplies?

....

....

....

Develop Possible Solutions

3. Collaborate with a partner to brainstorm possible solutions for your design that would meet the criteria and constraints. Write your ideas below.

....

....

....

Design It

4. Make a sketch of your virus design in the space below. Be sure to label the parts of the virus and their functions. Also, list the materials you will use to create the model.

Test and Evaluate Your Solution

5. Compare your design with those of other teams in your class. What materials did other teams use? How did the virus function? How did the team's design solve the problem differently from your design? In the space below, create two drawings that compare your design with another team's design. Label the differences and similarities.

Refine Your Solution

6. Based on your comparison with other teams, what problems do you still need to solve in your design? If you could improve your model, what would you do? Why?

....

....

....

....

7. Refine your model by incorporating your new ideas.

Communicate Your Solution

8. Present your completed design. Explain how the virus works and why you made the design decisions that you did. Discuss how evaluating other designs helped you refine your own model.

3

A Tree With Superpowers

Scientists at Harvard University are in early stages of development in making artificial leaves that mimic the photosynthetic factories growing on every tree you see. Like tree leaves, these manufactured leaves will absorb electromagnetic energy from the sun and produce chemical energy. The products of this artificial photosynthesis can then be used to provide energy as a fuel source for people to use. Ideally, the artificial leaves will be more efficient at producing energy for human uses than natural trees. They could be used wherever sunlight is abundant and where the soil quality is poor for plant growth.

Current artificial leaves look like small containers of clear liquid that absorb sunlight and produce energy. Assume that future developments will allow the process to occur in a flat sheet-like material. The surface of the material will absorb sunlight and provide a flow of electrical energy through a wire.

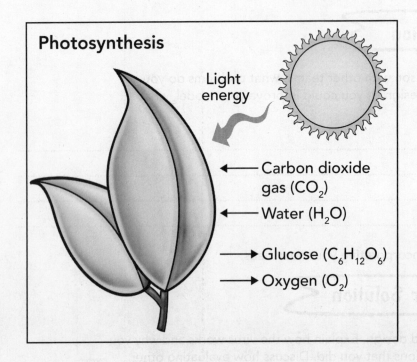

Photosynthesis

Light energy

← Carbon dioxide gas (CO_2)

← Water (H_2O)

→ Glucose ($C_6H_{12}O_6$)

→ Oxygen (O_2)

DESIGN CHALLENGE

You will design a structure that will hold artificial leaves and allow for the maximum flow of energy. One source of ideas for the design could be one that nature already uses – the tree. But you may want to think of new and innovative designs for structures that could be just as good or better than an artificial tree.

Define Your Problem

1. Your design must consider the size and shape of the artificial photosynthesis devices (the leaves) and how the devices are supported and arranged as they absorb energy from sunlight (the tree, bush, or other system). With your group, write a statement that defines the engineering problem you are trying to solve.

....

....

....

Identify Design Criteria/Constraints

2. In the table, write at least two criteria and two constraints that you need to consider when building an artificial tree. The criteria state what your design must accomplish. The constraints are the limitations on the solution. With your group, consider the goals of the project and likely limitations.

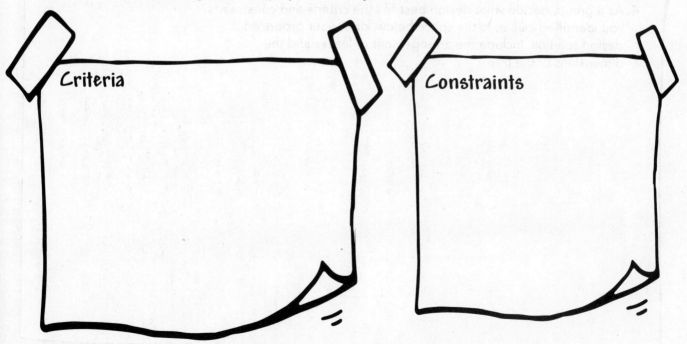

Criteria

Constraints

The Cell System • Engineering Design Notebook

Develop Possible Solutions

3. With your group, brainstorm possible designs of artificial trees. Consider the general shapes shown in the table and state at least one advantage and one disadvantage of each shape. Consider at least one additional shape of your choosing.

Tree Shape	Advantages	Disadvantages
Round	even distribution of leaves	leaves in center won't get enough sun
Spreading		
Pyramidal		

Design It

4. As a group, decide what design best fits the criteria and constraints you identified earlier. In the space below, draw your proposed design solution. Include the arrangement of leaves and the dimensions of the tree.

The Cell System • Engineering Design Notebook

5. Draw an image of the sun centered above your tree. Draw a straight line from the sun to the outer edge of your tree's top left branch. Then do the same with the top right branch. Imagine that the sun is hitting all the leaves within this triangular space. Is the sun hitting most of the leaves on your tree?

....

....

....

....

Communicate Your Solution

6. Make a poster or multimedia presentation that displays your artificial tree and demonstrates how it maximizes the amount of sunlight reaching the leaves. Compare your solution with that of other groups and note how the solutions differ from one another.

....

....

....

....

....

....

Refine Your Solution

7. After comparing your design to other designs, how could you change your tree to improve its performance?

....

....

....

....

....

Engineering an Organ

The cells, tissues, organs, and systems in your body all work together to keep you alive. For example, the respiratory system functions to bring oxygen into your body and remove carbon dioxide. The respiratory system does not do all this work alone, however. The system interacts with other body systems, such as the circulatory and muscular systems, to function properly.

Lungs are the major organs of the respiratory system. These organs are made up specialized cells that form different lung tissues. The structure of these tissues is related to their function. For example, the rigid tissue that makes up each bronchus helps to keep the airway open, allowing air to reach the bronchioles and alveoli. The flexible tissue of the lung lobes allows the organ to expand and contract as the diaphragm muscles push and pull on the lungs.

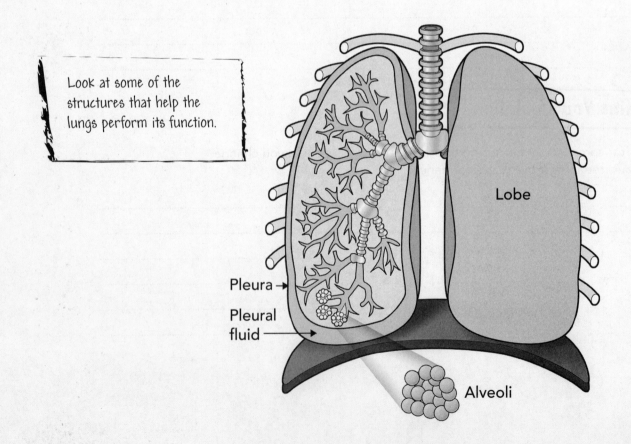

Look at some of the structures that help the lungs perform its function.

Lobe

Pleura →

Pleural fluid →

Alveoli

DESIGN CHALLENGE

Your school is hosting a healthy body initiative. Each class will develop and deliver a presentation on an organ in the human body that explains how it functions and how it works with other organs and systems in the body. Your class has been assigned the lung. As part of the presentation, you need to construct a simple model of a lung. The model should demonstrate how the structures of the lung function and how the organ interacts with other body systems.

Think about the different structures in the lung and how these parts work together. How you can replicate these structures and function with the materials supplied by your teacher. How functional will the model be? What parts will you need to duplicate? How will you test your model to make sure it functions properly?

Design Your Solution

1. With a partner, review the diagram of the lung and discuss how air enters and exits the organ. Make notes on the diagram to identify the important structures you need to consider during the construction process.

Think about whether you need to model all the structures of the lung or focus on the basic structures that will allow your model to function properly. Do you need to use all the materials available?

2. Your lung model must meet the following criteria and constraints.

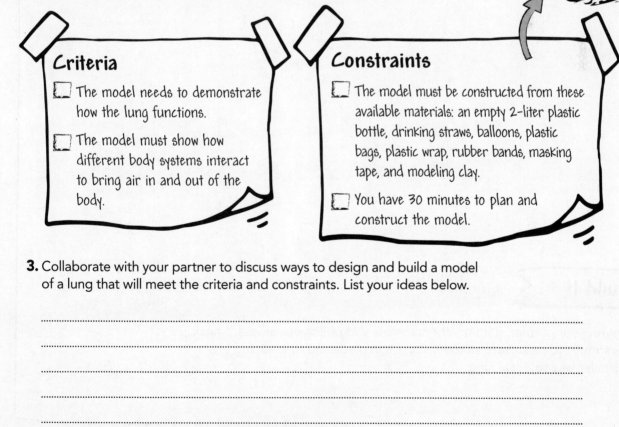

Criteria

☐ The model needs to demonstrate how the lung functions.

☐ The model must show how different body systems interact to bring air in and out of the body.

Constraints

☐ The model must be constructed from these available materials: an empty 2-liter plastic bottle, drinking straws, balloons, plastic bags, plastic wrap, rubber bands, masking tape, and modeling clay.

☐ You have 30 minutes to plan and construct the model.

3. Collaborate with your partner to discuss ways to design and build a model of a lung that will meet the criteria and constraints. List your ideas below.

....

....

....

....

....

Design It

4. Sketch your design in the space provided, showing how the model will look and how it will work. Your sketch should indicate the materials you will use and what purpose each will serve.

Build It

5. With your partner, gather your materials and build your model. Check carefully to make sure all the parts are in place and functioning in a similar way to a real lung.

Human Body Systems • Engineering Design Notebook

Evaluate Your Solution

6. When you have completed your model, present it to another team. Explain the solution you designed, and then demonstrate your model's functionality. Compare your design with the other team's design. How effectively do the designs show the structure and function of a real lung? What materials did the other team use? What might have made some of the team's design choices more or less effective than others?

....

....

....

....

Refine Your Solution

7. If you could improve the design of your model, how would you change it? Why?

....

....

....

....

8. Redesign your lung model to show the revisions. Then make the adjustments to your model.

Human Body Systems • Engineering Design Notebook

Build a Plant Growth Chamber

It has been more than forty years since humans walked on the moon. If astronauts were to go back to the moon, they might want to grow food so they could extend their stay. How would astronauts grow plants in the lunar environment?

The moon as an environment is very different from Earth, which means growing food there wouldn't be easy. For one thing, the amounts of light and radiation are very different. The moon also has a lesser force of gravity than Earth. This fact means that the effect gravity has on plants would be reduced on the moon.

Aside from light, plants need carbon dioxide, water, and nutrients These things would not be available from the lunar environment, so they need to be provided somehow by the lunar farmers.

In this activity, you will design and build a model of a lunar growth chamber. Your design must have features that provide what plants need to grow from seeds, including a proper environment. Your scale model does not need to be functional, but it should accurately depict how the growth chamber would work.

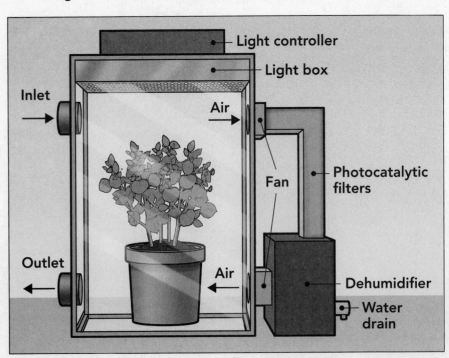

DESIGN CHALLENGE

Design and build a model of a lunar growth chamber that could be used to grow edible plants from seeds on the moon. The chamber must be connected to the larger moon base but it must be a separate, distinct unit that can be closed. The chamber can be no more than 15 square meters in area, and a minimum of 10 square meters of crops should be produced inside with sunlight being the only available source of light. The materials available for building a scale model are shown in the chart.

Before you begin, develop a clear statement of the problem you need to solve. The statement will help you identify the criteria and constraints that will inform your design.

Materials

- cardboard or foam-core board
- packing tape
- glue guns
- plastic wrap
- pins
- scissors
- dowels
- paper towels or filter paper
- plastic straws
- other materials provided by your teacher

Defining Your Problem

1. Based on what you have read about the environment on the moon, write an engineering problem statement for the project.

....

....

....

....

Identify Criteria and Constraints

2. List the criteria and constraints. Recall that criteria are things your project must feature or accomplish, while constraints are things that limit your design.

Criteria

- ☐ Chamber must be connected to main station, but be a distinct unit that can be closed
- ☐ Must produce at least 10 square meters of crops
- ☐ Must use sunlight

Constraints

- ☐ Chamber can't exceed 15 square meters in area
- ☐ Chamber can only use sunlight, no other light sources
- ☐ Weak force of gravity
- ☐ Very long periods with and without sunlight
- ☐ Lunar environment does not provide water, carbon dioxide, or nutrients

13

Design a Solution

3. Use the space below to sketch your design. Use labels to note the materials and their function in meeting the criteria while staying within the constraints.

Reproduction and Growth • Engineering Design Notebook

Build Your Solution

4. As a team, construct a model of your lunar growth chamber based on your sketch.

Communicate Your Solution

5. Present your model to the class, and describe how it would function in the lunar environment. Summarize your presentation below.

....

....

....

....

....

....

....

....

Refine Your Solution

6. After sharing your design with your classmates and hearing about their designs, propose one or more revisions to your lunar growth chamber design.

....

....

....

....

Put Decomposers to Work at Home

Think about all the waste that comes from your kitchen in a week. Where do those food scraps go? If you throw them in the trashcan, then they probably end up in a landfill. Yet this "waste" is a valuable resource. The plants in your garden need it. But you can't go out and toss food scraps in your garden.

To be useful, kitchen waste needs to be broken down into its basic elements. And the way to do this is through the process of composting. In composting, decomposers break down organic materials to form a nutrient-rich soil-like mix called compost.

Compost scientists describe the material going into the composter as brown and green. Brown materials such as paper, dried leaves, and wood chips are high in carbon and low in nitrogen. Green materials such as grass clippings and fruit or vegetable scraps are the opposite: high in nitrogen and low in carbon. A good compost mix needs both browns and greens in the right amounts, along with water and air. With the right compost, soil improves and a garden thrives.

In this large, outdoor composter, organic waste is added through a hole on top. Nitrogen-rich colorful waste such as fruit and vegetable scraps mix with the carbon-rich brown ingredients such as straw or dried leaves. Spinning the materials helps to expose them to air. Dark, rich compost exits from the side.

Drum composter

Organic waste

Brown and green waste mix together

Compost

DESIGN CHALLENGE

You have entered a design contest that challenges participants to build an effective home-scale composting system that can help to reduce the amount of household garbage sent to landfills.

Define the Problem

1. Define your engineering problem. Think about how much waste you need to process, how to control the smell, and what building materials you need. Now, write your engineering problem as a statement that describes what you want to accomplish. Research information about composters to help focus your work.

....

....

....

2. Add at least three additional criteria and three constraints that apply to your composter design.

Criteria

- ☐ composts a week's worth of kitchen waste—about 3 gallons
- ☐
- ☐
- ☐

Constraints

- ☐ must not produce offensive odors
- ☐
- ☐
- ☐

3. Using your list of criteria and constraints, decide on the key features your design should include. These features need to allow the composter to meet all of the criteria but not exceed the constraints.

....

....

....

Ecosystems and How They Change • Engineering Design Notebook

4. Make a sketch of your design. Label the materials that you will use and the dimensions of the composter. Also, include any features that are necessary to meet the criteria and constraints of the problem. An example of a feature might be holes in the lid and on the sides to allow more air to circulate.

Build a Solution

5. Use your sketch as a guide and build the composter.

Test and Evaluate Your Solution

6. Add the kitchen waste to the composter. Include any other materials that are needed, according to your research. Make and record observations every three days for three weeks.

Time	Temperature	Color	Odor	Other
Day 1				
Day 4				

7. What evidence would indicate that your prototype composter solves the problem while meeting the criteria and constraints?

....

....

....

....

8. After three weeks, evaluate the design of your composter. Evaluate your results in light of the criteria and constraints of the design problem, and compare with the results of other groups in your class. Include suggestions for improving the performance of your composter.

....

....

....

....

....

....

....

Communicate Your Solution

9. Present your design to the class. Include samples of your compost. Then, as a class, choose the team that did the best job of meeting the criteria while staying within the constraints.

Ecosystems and How They Change • Engineering Design Notebook

Building a Dome

The biomes at the Eden Project model the plant life found in two different biomes. A biome is a group of ecosystems with similar climates and organisms. The Rainforest biome is 55 m high, 100 m wide, 200 m long and covers 15,590 m^2. The Mediterranean biome is 35 m high, 65 m wide, and 135 m long, and covers about 6540 m^2.

Each biome structures is made of four interconnected geodesic domes. The design resembles soap bubbles that allow the structures to sit on the uneven clay pit surface. The geodesic domes are built on a steel framework made up of interconnecting triangles.

The frame for the biome domes is made of two layers. The outer layer is made of hexagons plus a pentagon. The inner layer has hexagons and triangles.

The design allows for maximum strength with a minimum amount of materials, maximum volume with minimal surface area, and no internal supports. To keep the structure lightweight, glass was not used for the windows. Instead, engineers used a new type of foil made of plastic. The foil was transparent, strong, lightweight, self-cleaning, a good insulator, and could last at least 25 years. To make the windows, three layers of foil were stretched over the steel framework.

Populations, Communities, and Ecosystems • Engineering Design Notebook

DESIGN CHALLENGE

Suppose you are hired to design a structure that will be used to showcase plant biodiversity in a biome, such as a desert or boreal forest. Consider what types of plants you would want to include in the biome and what space requirements they may have.

Design Your Solution

1. With your team, identify the type of biome your structure will represent. Your structure must accommodate plants that showcase a variety of shapes and sizes. Identify your biome below.

....

2. Your model of the biome structure must meet the following criteria and constraints.

Criteria

☐ Structure must be designed to house the greatest amount of plant biodiversity.

☐ Structure must be high enough to fit the tallest trees.

Constraints

☐ You have limited resources to work with to reduce costs.

☐ You have limited time to meet a strict deadline.

Use no more than 30 toothpicks and small clay balls

Spend no more than 25 minutes planning and building.

Collaborate with your team to discuss ways to design and build a model that will meet the criteria and constraints. List your ideas below.

....

....

....

....

....

....

3. Design your model below showing how your structure will use a maximum of 30 toothpicks and 15 small clay balls.

Build it

4. Using your sketch from above as a guide, build your model.

Evaluate Your Solution

5. Compare your model with those of other teams in your class. How did the other teams address size variations in their models? Describe why your team's model is a reasonable structure that meets all of the criteria and constraints.

....

....

....

....

....

....

....

Refine Your Solution

6. If you could improve your model, what would you change? Why?

....

....

....

....

....

....

....

7. Redesign your model below showing the changes.

8. If time allows, rebuild your model of the biome structure.

Develop a Secret Code

Secret messages have been around for a long time! Cryptography—the use of codes to protect secret information—was incorporated on clay tablets from Mesopotamia, dating back as far as 1500 B.C.E. In Egypt, codes were used even earlier. Today, texting is a code. It is an abbreviated form of language. Computer programmers write codes for software to perform functions such as playing a video or launching a website.

Codes can also be naturally occurring. DNA is the genetic information that provides information about traits such as hair and eye color, and blood type. The order of the base pairs A, T, G and C in DNA provides a code that specifies which type of protein will be made.

Codes require an algorithm, or key, to encode the original text. Computers enable users to engineer extremely sophisticated algorithms, but many types of codes require nothing more than pencil and paper. One example is the Pigpen code. It exchanges letters for symbols that are fragments of a grid.

Pigpen Code

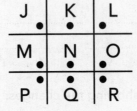

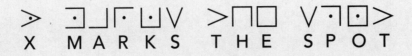

X MARKS THE SPOT

Genes and Heredity • Engineering Design Notebook

DESIGN CHALLENGE

Working as a cryptographer, you must design a secret code for use in transmitting classified information. The messages will be hand-carried and cannot rely on computers at either end. Think about what algorithm you will use. It needs a clear pattern so others can code and decode messages. Your engineering problem is to design an algorithm that is hard to solve just by guessing. An example of an algorithm that would not be suitable is A=1, B=2, C=3, and so on. This is a code that is very easy to break.

Identify Criteria and Constraints

1. Your design solution must meet these criteria and constraints.

Criteria

- ☐ The code includes a symbol for each letter of the alphabet.
- ☐ The decoding system must be easy for the recipient to use.
- ☐ The decoding system can be described in simple language or shown on a chart that can be rebuilt from memory.

Constraints

- ☐ The code cannot be so simple that it is easy to guess.
- ☐ Someone who knows the code can make a decoder.

Develop Possible Solutions

2. Collaborate with your group to develop ideas for a code that will meet the criteria and constraints. List your ideas below. Include at least two code ideas.

....

....

....

....

Genes and Heredity • Engineering Design Notebook

Design it

3. Choose the type of code that you will use. Describe what type of key you will use and how the recipient will decode a message when it is received.

....

....

....

....

4. Write the code key for the 26 letters of the alphabet on the lines.

....

....

....

....

....

....

....

Test Your Solution

5. With your group, create several encrypted sentences using your code. Each partner should create one sentence; then you should exchange sentences and try to decode your partner's sentence. This will help you check for flaws in your code and make sure your code isn't too complex. Record the results of your test.

....

....

....

....

....

....

....

Genes and Heredity • Engineering Design Notebook

6. Test the security and the usability of your code. Write a two-sentence message using the code. Exchange messages with another group. To test security, try to decode each other's messages within ten minutes without knowing the key. Test usability by describing the code key so that the other group can reproduce it. Then have each group develop a key and decode the message. Record your observations.

....
....
....
....
....
....
....
....
....
....
....

Refine Your Solution

7. If you could improve your code, how would you change it? Why?.

....
....
....
....
....
....
....
....
....
....
....
....
....

Way to Dig!

Archaeologists investigate the history of people and their activities. Part of their mission is preserving objects that link us to history. A piece of broken pottery or a worn out, discarded tool often best tells the story of the culture that once inhabited a place.

Many of these pieces of the past are buried in soil, clay, or even rock. They are old and often very fragile. Archaeologists need a variety of tools to carefully remove artifacts from their surroundings and scrape away material adhering to them. Each researcher has favorite tools. The main goal is to isolate the artifact without harming it. Archaeologists tools could include:

- Shovels for digging quickly and moving soil

- Trowels for careful digging and getting into tight spaces

- Screens and sieves to separate objects from loose soil

- Picks made of wood, bamboo, or metal to move small amounts of soil

- Tape measures to record exact locations of objects at the site

- Brushes and dustpans to remove fine soil and dust

Although there are manufacturers who make tools specifically for the tasks that archaeologists do in the field, many tools are made by modifying something made for another purpose.

Archaeologists may use common tools for their work in the field or they may develop a tool to fit their specific needs.

DESIGN CHALLENGE

Using the tools provided by your teacher, carefully recover whatever artifacts might be buried in the tray of soil given to your group. Use care not to damage the artifacts that you are recovering. Once you can see the artifact, take photographs of the artifact in the soil before you remove it.

Now, based on your experience in recovering artifacts in soil, design a tool that a paleontologist or archaeologist could use to remove a fragile fossil or artifact without harming it. You can design a tool that a toolmaker would manufacture or a tool that someone could make using items available at a store. Then you will explain how your design would be used at a dig site.

Define the Problem

1. Imagine working at a dig site looking for small fragile pieces of fossilized bone or broken pottery. Consider your experience with finding buried objects. What kind of tool could you use to excavate a site while protecting artifacts? Does your tool need to move a lot of soil quickly? Does it need to reach into tight spots? Does it need to be easy to carry up a steep slope? Think about the characteristics a good tool would need to have to be useful in the field.

   Your tool can address any part of the task of recovering the artifact. Now write a clearly defined engineering problem that states what the tool you need to use will do and how you will use it.

   ....

   ....

   ....

   ....

   ....

   ....

   ....

   ....

2. Consider the key points of your design problem. Use the Internet to research tools that scientists use now. Is there a way to improve on current tools?

Now think about the limits on your design. Make a list of two criteria and constraints that your design must address.

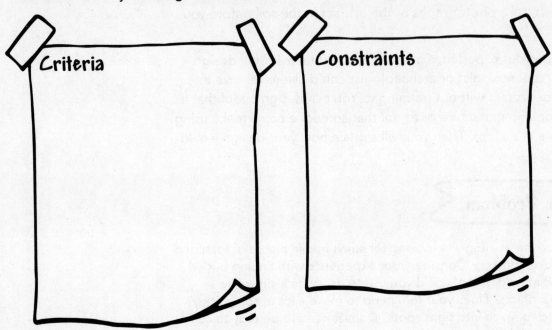

Criteria

Constraints

Develop Possible Solutions

3. Consider the criteria and constraints that you have listed. Propose a possible design that might meet the criteria and the constraints. Write a description of your design, stating what materials the tool will be made of and how it will function at the dig site.

....

....

....

....

....

....

....

....

....

Design It

4. Sketch what your design will look like. Label the parts and state what materials will be used in each part.

Communicate Your Solution

5. Present your final design solution to your class. Explain how your tool will address a specific need that was described in your design problem. Listen to feedback about ways that you could refine the solution. Give constructive feedback to other class members when they present their solutions.